TRACTORS

TRACTORS

STEPHEN RICHMOND & JONATHAN WHITLAM

FARMING PRESS

Front cover

Two 130hp MASSEY FERGUSON 6190 tractors harvesting potatoes.

Frontispiece

A 103hp VALMET 8400 pulls away from the combine with a trailer load of wheat.

Back cover

A 110hp John Deere 6600 poses alongside a 95hp FORD 7740.

First published 1998

Copyright © Stephen Richmond & Jonathan Whitlam 1998

All rights reserved. No part of this publication may be reproduced, stored in a retrieval system, or transmitted, in any form or by any means, electronic, mechanical, photocopying, recording or otherwise, without prior permission of Farming Press.

ISBN 0 85236 517 9

A catalogue record for this book is available from the British Library

**Published by Farming Press
Miller Freeman UK Ltd
Wharfedale Road, Ipswich, IP1 4LG
United Kingdom**

Distributed in North America by Diamond Farm Enterprises Box 537, Bailey Settlement Road Alexandria Bay, NY 13607, USA

Origination and printing by TSS Digital, Margate, Kent

The tractor is the most important piece of equipment on the farm. It helps to plough, sow, harvest and transport the crop away from the field. Various implements can be attached to the front or back of the tractor to carry out two jobs at once and some tractors can carry hoppers or tanks as well. Today there is no job on the farm that at least one type of tractor cannot carry out easily.

In this book we take a look at a small selection of the many different makes and models that are available today. We have tried to include some of the most popular models as these are the tractors that you are most likely to see at work out in the fields.

The 'ABOUT THE TRACTOR' boxes give some of the more important details about each tractor model featured in the photographs. We have tried to keep it as simple as possible, but to make it easier to follow this is what the different headings mean.

Model Number	Easy this one! The number used to identify a particular tractor.
Engine Size	The power of the tractor's engine in horsepower (hp).
Number of Cylinders	This is the number of cylinders the tractor has. The cylinders are the heart of the engine and usually, the bigger the engine, the more cylinders it will have.
Number of Gears	Every tractor has a different type of gearbox which transfers the power from the engine to the wheels, and this varies from model to model. In our boxes the first number tells you the number of forward gears a tractor has while the second is the number of reverse gears.
Top Speed	Another easy one! The fastest speed the tractor can go.
Weight	How heavy the tractor is, usually without added extras, in kilograms (kg).

These figures should only be used as a rough guide. The tractors you see out in the fields may be fitted with different gearboxes or more powerful engines. This is because manufacturers are continually changing and improving their tractors, something that means they will never become boring! Happy reading and happy tractor hunting!

John Deere 6000 Series

ABOUT THE TRACTOR

Model Number	6400
Engine Size	100hp
Number of Cylinders	4
Number of Gears	24 x 24
Top Speed	25mph
Weight	4100kg

The JOHN DEERE 6400, shown round baling, is fitted with a front-mounted frame to which a hoe for weeding sugar beet can be attached. It is also equipped with narrow tyres, ideal for work in-between growing crops. The largest tractor in the range is the 130hp 6900. The inside of the cab of this tractor is shown on the left. The 6000 Series tractors are made in Germany.

Case IH Magnum PRO

Made in America, the MAGNUM 7250 PRO is the largest in the CASE IH MAGNUM range. When heavy implements, such as ploughs and cultivators, are attached to the back of the tractor large weights are carried on the tractor's front frame to help keep the front wheels on the ground. This also helps the tractor to gain more grip. The smallest MAGNUM is the 171hp 7210 PRO.

ABOUT THE TRACTOR

Model Number	7250
Engine Size	272hp
Number of Cylinders	6
Number of Gears	24 x 6
Top Speed	25mph
Weight	8950kg

Deutz-Fahr Agrotron

ABOUT THE TRACTOR

Model Number	130
Engine Size	142hp
Number of Cylinders	6
Number of Gears	24 x 24
Top Speed	25mph
Weight	5360kg

The DEUTZ-FAHR AGROTRON range is built in Germany by Italian firm SAME DEUTZ-FAHR. It has a sharply sloping bonnet and very thin side pillars that allow the driver a clear view all round the tractor. The rear view shows the three-point linkage to which implements are attached. Below these there is a pick-up hitch for towing trailers and other trailed equipment.

Lamborghini Racing

ABOUT THE TRACTOR

Model Number	165
Engine Size	165hp
Number of Cylinders	6
Number of Gears	27 x 27
Top Speed	25mph
Weight	5830kg

LAMBORGHINI tractors are made in Italy by SAME DEUTZ-FAHR. This RACING 165 is fitted with a front linkage as well as the main at the rear. This means that the tractor can be fitted with implements at the front as well as the back. The smaller picture shows the larger 189hp RACING 190 with a seed hopper on its front linkage and a power harrow/drill combination unit on the rear.

JCB Fastrac

ABOUT THE TRACTOR

Model Number	1135
Engine Size	135hp
Number of Cylinders	6
Number of Gears	36 x 12
Top Speed	31mph
Weight	5300kg

JCB FASTRACs are capable of a much faster road speed than ordinary tractors and are fitted with air-operated brakes and a suspension system that gives the driver a smoother ride. A space behind the tractor cab allows for the fitting of fertiliser hoppers and spray tanks. This 1135 is also fitted with the QUADTRONIC four-wheel steering system, which means this equal-size wheeled tractor can turn tightly at the end of the field.

Massey Ferguson 6100 Series

ABOUT THE TRACTOR

Model Number	6170
Engine Size	110hp
Number of Cylinders	6
Number of Gears	32 x 32
Top Speed	24mph
Weight	4655kg

As with many modern tractors, this MASSEY FERGUSON 6170 is fitted with front mudguards, which help stop mud and water spraying up on to the cab windows, and a side-mounted exhaust stack which helps to improve the driver's forward view. A number of powerful worklights, mounted on both the front and back of the tractor cab, makes working in the dark easier.

Valmet 6000 Series

The VALMET 6400 is made in Finland and is available, like all VALMET tractors, in either red, blue, white, yellow or green. The larger 115hp 6800, which has a side-mounted exhaust next to the cab instead of the bonnet-mounted exhaust on the 6400, is shown.

ABOUT THE TRACTOR

Model Number	6400
Engine Size	95hp
Number of Cylinders	4
Number of Gears	24 x 24
Top Speed	25mph
Weight	4170kg

New Holland 60 Series

ABOUT THE TRACTOR

Model Number	8260
Engine Size	115hp
Number of Cylinders	6
Number of Gears	18 x 6
Top Speed	25mph
Weight	5250kg

The NEW HOLLAND 60 Series tractors are made in Britain, with the FORD tractors in blue and the identical specification M Series FIATAGRI tractors in brown. It has large wing mirrors, a large opening rear window and the worklights are positioned on the rear mudguard. The smaller picture shows the biggest in the range, the 160hp 8560.

Claas Challenger

ABOUT THE TRACTOR

Model Number	55
Engine Size	270hp
Number of Cylinders	6
Number of Gears	16 x 9
Top Speed	18mph
Weight	9977kg

The CLAAS CHALLENGER 55 is made in Canada by CATERPILLAR where it is sold in the yellow CAT colours, as you can see in the smaller photograph. In Europe it is sold by CLAAS of Germany. An alternative to wheeled tractors, the rubber tracks spread its weight while also giving the tractor more grip in wet conditions.

To find out more about tractors and other farm machinery contact:

**Farming Press
Miller Freeman UK Ltd
2 Wharfedale Road, Ipswich, IP1 4LG
United Kingdom
Tel: (+ 44) 01473 241122**

Frogs and Toads

Experts on child reading levels
have consulted on the level of text and
concepts in this book.

At the end of the book is a "Look Back and Find" section
which provides additional information and encourages
the child to refer back to previous pages
for the answers to the questions posed.

Angela Grunsell trained as a teacher in 1969.
She has a Diploma in Reading and Related Skills
and for the last five years has advised London
teachers on materials and resources.
She worked for the ILEA as an
advisory teacher and is currently
teaching in a primary school in Hackney, London.

Published in Great Britain in 1985 by
Franklin Watts, 12a Golden Square, London W1

© Aladdin Books Ltd/Franklin Watts

Designed and produced by
Aladdin Books Ltd, 70 Old Compton Street, London W1

ISBN 0 86313 314 2

Printed in Belgium

FRANKLIN · WATTS · FIRST · LIBRARY

Frogs and Toads

by
Kate Petty

Consultant
Angela Grunsell

Illustrated by
Alan Baker

Franklin Watts
London · New York · Toronto · Sydney

Which is the frog and which is the toad?
This one is the Common Frog. It is about five centimetres long.

Its shiny skin is a greenish colour.

It can leap a long way on its strong back legs.

The Common Toad has a brown, warty skin. It is usually bigger than a frog, with a broader back. Unlike frogs, toads walk rather slowly. They come out mostly at night.

A mother frog lays 2,000 eggs, called frogspawn. The father holds her so that he can fertilize the eggs as soon as they are laid. The eggs look like little dots in a mass of jelly.

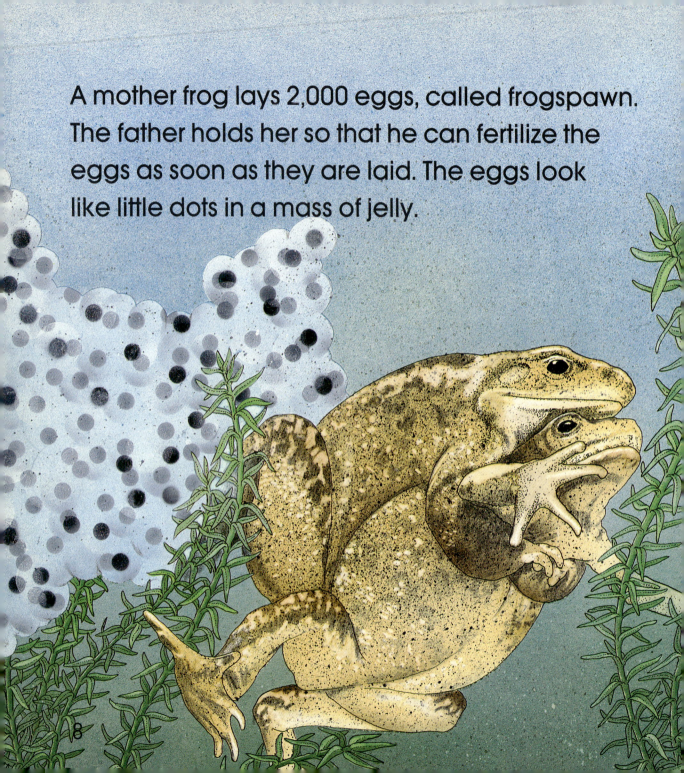

Can you see how different toadspawn looks? About 4,000 eggs are laid in ribbons which wrap themselves around the water plants. Toads and frogs nearly always lay their eggs in water.

When the eggs hatch, thousands of tiny, wriggly tadpoles emerge from the jelly. Only a very few will survive long enough to become frogs. Other pond creatures like to eat tadpoles.

A tadpole lives in the water like a fish. It breathes oxygen through the gills on the side of its head. It moves by flicking its tail. Small tadpoles feed off algae and pondweed.

Frogs and toads grow bigger in the same way. They are getting ready for life out of the water. By eight weeks the Common Toad tadpole has lungs for breathing air and a pair of back legs.

This little creature is really beginning to look like a frog.
At twelve weeks it has front legs with "hands" and its tail is already shorter.

A baby frog is called a froglet. When it is strong enough it hops out of the water onto the land. Its powerful back legs with webbed feet are good for swimming too.

A full-grown frog is amphibious. This means that it can live on land and in water.
A frog never lives too far away from water as it needs to keep its skin moist.

A frog has eyes in the top of its head. It can peep out of the water without being seen. Frogs blink when they swallow. Their eyeballs push against their mouths to help the food down.

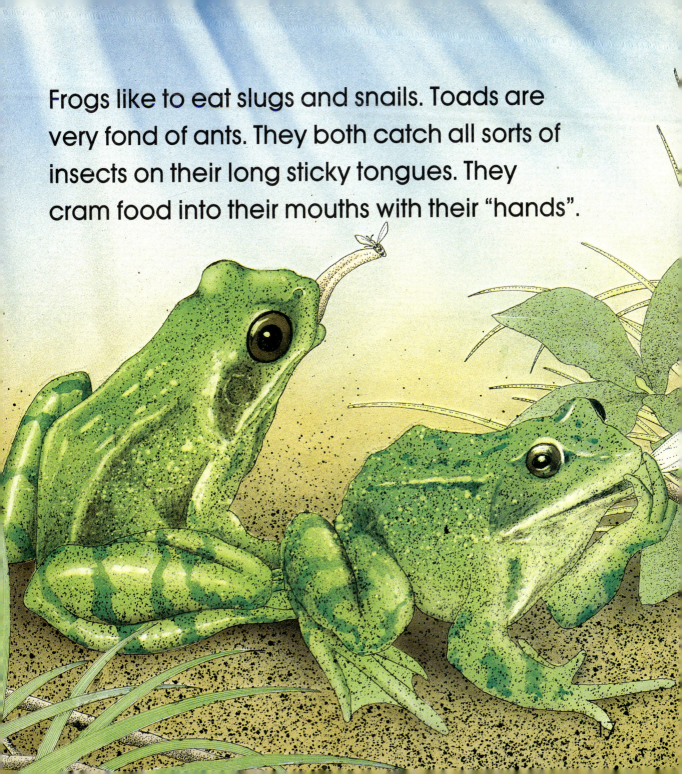

Frogs like to eat slugs and snails. Toads are very fond of ants. They both catch all sorts of insects on their long sticky tongues. They cram food into their mouths with their "hands".

Have you ever heard frogs or toads croaking? Some of them don't make much noise but this American Reed Frog can be heard a long way off. He puffs out his throat like a balloon.

Only the male frogs and toads can croak.
They are calling and singing to their mates.
They can even croak under water.
This is a Marine Toad from Central America.

A frightened frog can puff up its whole body. It puts its hands over its eyes and draws in its back legs. This makes it harder for another animal to grab hold of it.

Toads can make themselves look much bigger to scare off enemies. They can change colour slightly so that it is harder to see them. Some toads and frogs can make their skins poisonous.

There are over 2,600 different frogs and toads. Many of them are brightly coloured and live in tropical countries, like these little climbing Tree Frogs from Central America.

Wallace's Flying Frog from Malaya
can glide from tree to tree.
Its webbed feet are like parachutes.
The Reed Frog from East Africa climbs up reeds.

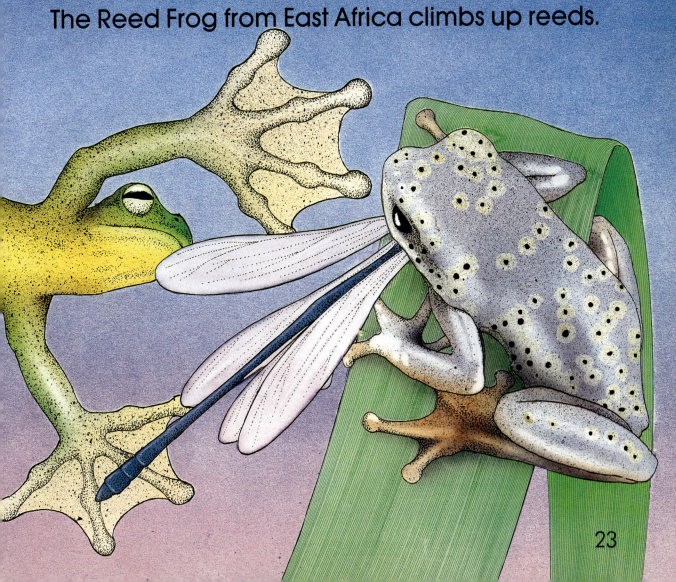

The male European Midwife Toad wraps the spawn around his legs and carries it about. The Firebelly Toad from Central America shows by its warning markings that is it poisonous.

When the Spadesfoot Toad from the Plains of Central America is in danger it just sinks from view, quietly digging a hole with its back feet.

Most frogs and toads go to sleep for the winter. Frogs stay damp in the mud but you might find a toad sleeping in a barn or a cellar. In spring they go back to their ponds to mate.

Every spring thousands of toads cross busy roads on their way back. Helpers sometimes lift them across in buckets so that they can reach their breeding ponds in safety.

Look back and find

At what time of year do you find frogspawn?
In early spring.

What is the best way to study tadpoles?
It is always best to study wildlife in its own habitat, but you can take a cupful of spawn and a little weed. Keep it in a large aquarium filled with tap water.

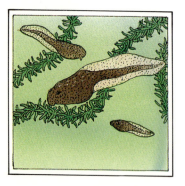

What do tadpoles eat in captivity?
In the first two weeks the tadpoles can get all they need from the weed and a few boiled nettles. Then you can feed them on a little fish food. Remember to change half the water once a week. Once their back legs are fully formed you should return them to the pond where their natural diet helps them to grow into frogs.

How do baby frogs and toads get ready for land?

What happens to the tadpole's tail?
It gets shorter and shorter and eventually disappears.

What is this toad doing?

Can all frogs and toads change colour?
Most frogs and some toads can change colour. The Common Frog can be a different colour each time you see it, switching between green and brown to match its surroundings.

Can frogs fly?
Not really. Wallace's Flying Frog takes a tremendous leap and glides from one tree to another.

Where does this frog come from?

What is special about its feet?

What is the Firebelly doing?

Would you be poisoned if you touched its skin?
No, not unless you had cut yourself. Even the Common Toad will make an unpleasant juice come from its skin if it is frightened.

Index

A American Reed Frog 18
amphibious 15

B breathing

C colour 6, 7, 21, 22, 24
Common Frog 6
Common Toad 7, 12
croaking 18, 19

E eating 11, 16, 17
eggs 8, 9, 10
eyes 16

F feet 14, 25
Firebelly Toad 24
froglet 14
frogspawn 8

G gills 11

H hands 13, 17, 22

L leap 6, 14
legs 6, 12, 14, 25
lungs 12, 13

M Marine Toad 19
Midwife Toad 25
mouth 16, 17

P poison 21, 24
puffing up 20, 21

R Reed Frogs 18, 23
roads 27

S skin 6, 7, 15, 21
sleep 11
Spadesfoot Toad 25
swimming 14

T tadpoles 10, 11, 12
tail 11, 13
toadspawn 9, 25
tongue 17
Tree Frog 22

W Wallace's Flying Frog 23
webbed feet 14, 23

BEYOND SWAT

Reconciliation: what is needed now

By the time I interviewed these women, four months had elapsed since most people who had fled Swat had returned. I could see signs of rebuilding—mostly by using private funds, but much was also being renovated by the army. It was very clear that the military's ongoing presence was important to these women. They had lived very sheltered lives cared for by fathers, husbands, brothers, and sons, many of whom were no longer there. For the women, the role of protector was being shouldered by the military. Importantly, too, the military's ongoing presence for these women—perhaps not for men in the area, but for these women—shows that the state cares about its people, and that the people can rely on the state. A woman said to me, "Be grateful for what you have now. Because of the army, things are OK."

But for how long can militancy be fought only by the military? There is no concerted effort, other than the military's presence, to offset the influence of the Swat Taliban. The army sent out a notice to all traders that shutters in the bazaar had to be painted with the Pakistan flag, a reminder that militarism remains a potent threat but also that Swat is a part of Pakistan. However the legal system has not changed, nor are there many new jobs, "The biggest effect of the Taliban was on the poor. There are no jobs, not even for educated people." The Pakistan government's efforts to run periodic "tourist sales" in Swat, even giving away hotel

Figure 13.4: Pakistan flags painted on shutters in all Swat bazaars.